Who Did Th[c

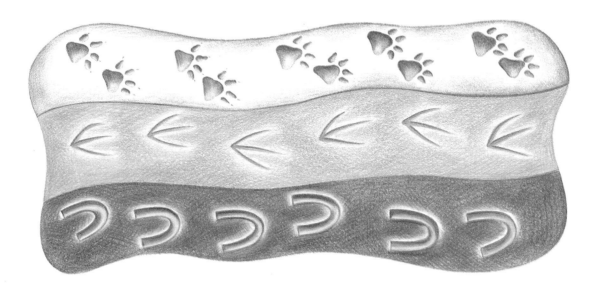

Written by Christine Harris
Illustrated by Isabel Rayner

Collins Educational
An imprint of HarperCollins*Publishers*

Who made paw prints
in the snow?

I did!

Who made claw prints in
the sand?

I did!

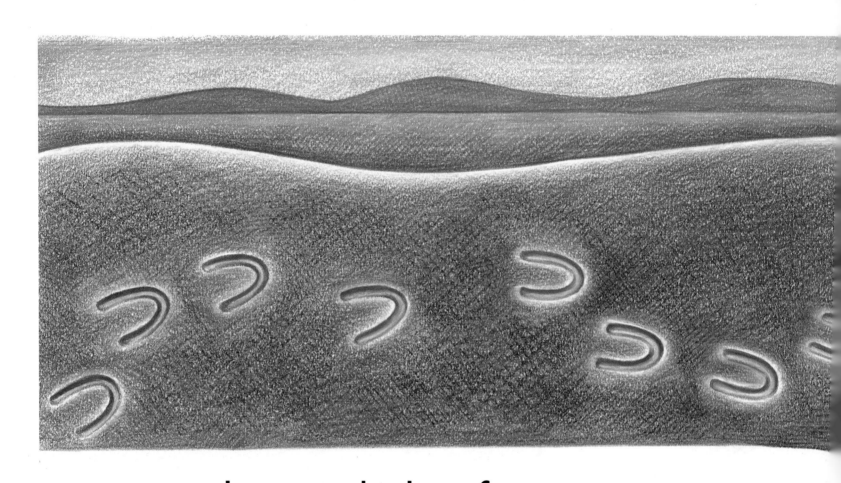

Who made hoof prints in
the mud?

I did!

Who made footprints on the floor?

I didn't!